All Kinds of Teams

by Bonnie Ferraro

Table of Contents

Chapter 1

What Is a Team?

A team is a group of people who work together. The people on a team help each other. This team works hard to sell lemonade. People will pay money to buy these drinks. This team will also have fun.

This team works together at home.

This team waters the plants in a garden.

People can be on teams at home, at school, and in their **community**. This team works together in a community garden. They take care of the plants.

Chapter 2
Teams at Home

A family is one kind of team. In a family, everyone can help with the meals. This family shops at the store. They will buy food to cook and eat at home.

It is a lot of fun to shop as a team.

This family team cooks a big pot of sauce with ripe tomatoes.

In a family, one person may cook the meal. Someone else may set the table. After dinner, other family members may wash the dishes and clean up.

This mother shows her children how to cook.

Ben and Joan are brother and sister. They like working in the yard.

The people in this family team up to clean their yard. They use rakes to gather the leaves that have fallen and blown around. Then they will put the leaves into a garbage bag. Later someone else will mow the lawn.

Working in the yard can be a difficult job.

Most pets need a lot of care.
A family can work as a team
to take care of their pet, too.

One person can be **responsible** for
feeding the dog. Everyone can take
turns walking the dog.

This brother and sister give their dog a bath.
Joe makes sure the dog doesn't move, while
Leah rinses off the soap.

Chapter 3
Teams at School

This boy acts in a school play.

At school, students can be on different teams. Some students put on plays. They act and move around the stage. Putting on a play takes a big team!

The students on the team must build sets and make costumes. They must help each other learn their parts, too.

Have you ever been on a team that put on a play?

These children paint sets for a play.

These children play flutes in the school band.

Many students play instruments in a school band. They have to practice often so they can play better. A **conductor** leads this music-making team.

Other students play on sports teams. They pick the sport that they like best, such as soccer or basketball, and join the team. A person called a **coach** teaches them how to play. Everyone has to learn the rules of the game. They also have to practice together.

These children play on soccer teams.

Chapter 4

Teams in the Community

This team plants flowers in the park.

People in a community also form teams. They work together to change their community. They want to make it a better place to live.

Some community teams take care of other people. Some people make meals and bring them to their **neighbors**. Others visit people who are sick.

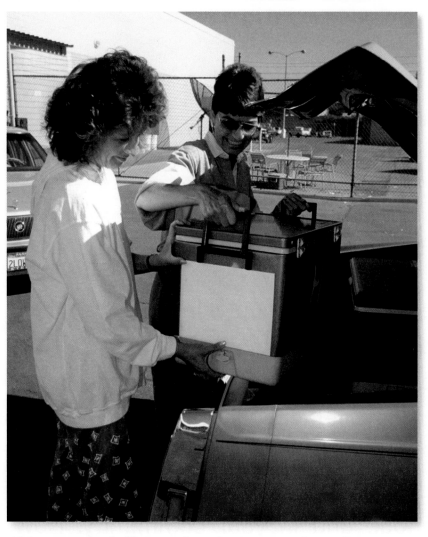

This team delivers food to people who are sick.

Chapter 5

Why Are Teams Important?

This team works together at home.

There are many reasons to join a team. When people join teams, they can feel that they are a part of something special. They learn how to work together, and they have fun, too.

You can be on a team at home, at school, and in your community. Now is the time to join in and show what you can do.

Glossary

coach *(KOHCH)* a person who teaches people who play sports *(page 11)*

community *(kuh-MYEW-ni-tee)* a group a people who live and work together *(page 3)*

conductor *(kuhn-DUK-TUHR)* a person who leads a band or orchestra *(page 10)*

neighbor *(NAY-buhr)* a person who lives near you *(page 13)*

responsible *(ri-SPON-suh-buhl)* to have a job or duty *(page 7)*

Index

Comprehension Check

Retell

Use the Retell Chart to help you tell what you learned from this book.

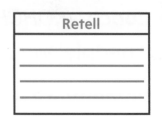

Think and Compare

1. Look back at pages 4 and 5. How do families work as a team?

2. What teams have you been on? What did you do to help the team?

3. What are some ways team members can make their team better?